The Swallows

The Swallows

poems by
Adriana E. Ramírez

BLUE SKETCH PRESS | PITTSBURGH

THE SWALLOWS. 2nd edition. Copyright © 2016 by Adriana E. Ramírez. Originally published by Blue Sketch Press in 2014. All rights reserved including right of reproduction in whole or in part or in any form. For information, address Blue Sketch Press, 1124 De Victor Pl., Pittsburgh, PA 15206.

"The Naming Things" was previously published in Aster(ix) Journal, 2013.
"Politica" previously published in HEArtOnline , 2013.
Printed with permission from author.

www.bluesketchpress.com
www.facebook.com/bluesketchpress.com

The Swallows
by Adriana E. Ramírez — 2nd ed.
    ISBN (print)   978-1-942547-03-7 (trade paperback)

Cover Art by George Lu, "Swallow"
More information available at www.flickr.com/photos/gzlu
Design by Little Owl Creative, www.littleowlcreative.com
Edited by Joseph N. Welch, III.

Second Edition: March 2016

Printed in the United States of America
9 8 7 6 5 4 3 2 1

Contents

Chiles Rellenos	9
Daughter of the American Revolution	11
Plastic	15
Azteca	16
The Heretic's Guide to Living with Gingivitis	18
Politica	20
Little Nutty Bar	22
The Airplane Wife	25
the origins of the knife war	28
the end of the knife war	29
For Libertad	30
Joan Miró Stares at the Harvest Moon	34
In Which I Tell You About My Morning	36
Ivy	38
dog and bird discuss flight, what dog remembers	40
Bird and Dog Discuss Taste, What Bird Remembers	41

The Celia Cruz Cycle	42
gravity and disappointment	50
Things I Wish Weren't True #1	51
Things I Wish Weren't True #2	53
Tlaloc (Casa Frida Kahlo, March 2001)	56
glitterati	57
Deboradora	59
Icarus	61
Eff Mi	65
The Naming of Things	68
A Simile Like You	72
How to Punch Someone Without Getting Hurt	76
It's a Doggy Dog World	80
About the Author	83

For Maria Josefina Benitez de Ramírez
9/8/1922 – 2/18/2014

Chiles Rellenos

Alba makes Chiles Rellenos for the first time.
Twenty-six years old, sweating, grunting.

Pinches Mexicanos.
Que humor, llenar estas
vainas con carne y queso.

She will go on like for the next hour,
not because she hates Mexicans,
but because she's using the wrong peppers.

When finished, a feast:
thirty tiny Serrano Peppers, fiery pea-shells,
one twentieth the size of the Poblanos they emulate,
filled with carne molida and Oaxaca cheese.

Not an easy battle, hunched over the table,
surgically slicing and stuffing, eyebrow-plucking
mirror transformed into a chile-stuffing necessity.
The baby laughs at her in the corner.

Alba will pick up the phone, stand erect behind the

THE SWALLOWS

counter, slam buttons like a judge
does a gavel, and softly say to the receiver:
I made you Chiles Rellenos. Like you always want.

Alex will come home, kiss his wife, and marvel at her work.
He will eat every last chile, not saying a word.
Meat and cheese overcome by burning,
he will not ask for water.
Alba sits and watches him,
bouncing the baby on her knee, pleased.
When the meal is over, she will wash his plate,
and hum a cumbia, waiting for Alex's verdict.

Gracias, mi amor.
Estaba muy rico.

Alex cracks open a beer, Alba sits beside him.
They watch television from the kitchen table,
holding hands underneath.

Daughter of the American Revolution

I almost failed my citizenship test.
There were ten questions;
I missed the first two.

To be fair, I was twelve, and I
explicitly told the old lady administrator
I faired poorly on dates.

My first lesson as an American:
Exposing weakness merely opens you up to attack.

My friend Matilda will slough
the skin of slavery over coffee too often.
Four hundred years, intoned reverent.

The goal, she will explain,
is to miscegenate things just.
The future looks like you—

this is when she will point at me,

melting pot of wrongs made right.

What day was the Constitution signed?
A trick question, designed to confuse.
Most people answer Fourth of July.

I know this because I will, for years,
poll my US American friends.
All of them miss the question.

I have committed the date to memory,
perfect in my acquired patriotism.

Matilda laughs when I tell her I'm more
American than she. *Not Possible*, she'll say.
And I'll know she's capitalized the letters.

I am a daughter of Africa, Europe, and America.
I tell her I am the same. A different Africa,
a different Europe, a different America.

Plus, she'll say, *I was born here.*
I'm not sure that counts as much as she thinks.

The second question I miss:

Adriana E. Ramírez

What day did the Civil War end?
I mishear it and answer "slavery."

The old lady will repeat the question
charitable in her administration.
"Appomattox" I will respond.

She'll repeat "day" like I'm deaf,
until I circle my head slowly,
in disbelief that sounds like Spanish.

I will grow tired of Matilda.
Her contests about what shade of brown
had it worse will wear me thin.

I will try to explain the plight of Latin
America. Raped by conquistadores, double
raped by America's Monroe Acquisitions Act.

I will tell her there's nothing more American,
than naming yourself after an entire continent,
as if there was no one else, *United States of.*

I'll ask her if she knows the date of Appomattox.
My smugness doesn't fit inside her silence.

When I swore to be a US American,

The Swallows

I was given a flag pin and a letter of welcome
from the Daughters of the American Revolution.

I looked at this old woman, so different from the one before,
hugging me in congratulations,
as if she'd given me the keys to heaven.

"September 17, 1787," I said to her.
She smiled, confused. "April 9th, 1865."
She nodded and mouthed, *of course, dearie.*

As if her father's revolution was a secret I kept.
She simply delivered flags and soft hugs—
a legacy of stick-waving and heart-palming.

And to Matilda, I will say,
*I took a test to be here. I filled out forms,
waited in lines, endured examinations—*

*I wanted it. Don't you see, Matilda,
I wanted it
unlike you.*

As if that counts for anything at all.

Plastic

She asks me if I'll consider plastic surgery.
Get myself a thigh gap and a Shakira belly.
Remove the skin beneath my chin,
streamline my ass and make my lips more kissable.

I find my face within my mother's.
My father's eyes look out my head.
I enjoy commiserating about our propensities,
the dispositions that make us who we are.

I'm afraid to succumb; perhaps because I don't believe
in non-medical surgery. Not the way I don't believe
in Santa Claus, but in the way I don't believe in my
ex-boyfriends' smiles and old love letters:

Some promises leave bigger scars than knives.

Azteca

There is power in blood.

Blood pulls the obsidian out of hiding.
Blood sings to the mirror god.
Blood honors the jaguar.

When you untether a child
at dawn, the sun kisses earth—
thanks the empty wombs, uses its
newfound youth to appease
the cooler veins.

The knife will lick the torso clean.
The handle will be feathered.
The stone will be polished a human shade of red.

If she cries at the altar,
the rain will fall sooner.

If he dies with a sceptre,
the battle will win quickly.

Adriana E. Ramírez

If we bleed our enemies enough,
we'll learn to love them more for it—

They've given us so much.

We are forgiven in the evening with each breath.
We prepare to surrender our own flesh as offering.
We sacrifice, we worship, we submit.

We light small bodies on fire,
so the rest of us will never burn.

We cut open hearts,
so our own will not stop beating.

Blood is how the gods listen.
Blood is the opposite of death.
Blood is what we make to live.

The Heretic's Guide to Living with Gingivitis

Only two things terrify me—
and I think Jesus is self-explanatory.
The other is my teeth falling out.

I read on the internet this is a common terror,
something we all share that transcends kind:
we fear grandpa's dentures.
The gaping hole where knives once lived.
The beast declawed and capped.

Bleeder, my dentist baptized me,
as if my molars plotted against her.
I pled good regimen—
burning mouthwash and righteous flossing—
and she pointed out that some folks are just Bleeders.
Like menstruation and stigmata,
gums remind me of the holy within the body.
Except I swallow the rust of nails,
taste the iron and saw.

I could handle the tooth part of detachment.
I am not so vowed to bone that I cannot replace it.

No, my fear is what remains—
raw-nerved hole, denuded.
My tongue hesitant in exploration,
the Thomas-doubt of flesh manifest;
I lick my wounds too often for them to heal clean.

How I am a bad Catholic:
the Jesus in my bedroom is abstract.
Wrought aluminum, stick-figured,
haloed on walnut.
Lean on his cross,
shiny like a dentist's pick.

Pure like a nightmare.

Politica

A body washed ashore that summer,
bullet-riddled in fatigues.
We gathered around, five cousins,
bold and bored from days at the beach.
The youngest joked that fish made
dinner of the dead man's eyes.
Two strangers nodded and my cousin vomited.

Colombia, when I miss you,
I try to think of days like this: when guerilla death
tolls tell better stories than grandmothers.
Days like sand, children, and a blind man
petrified in his prayer.

Days like my American passport: blue, godhead, imperial—
pretenses of immunity and power
ready to be stripped by a soldier,
a boy who knows accents do not identify
corpses like blood. A boy whose gun
escorts my mother, date for interrogation,
the last step before flight.
She'll board with me, free of her homeland,

always afraid of turning to salt.

But televised outcries never cease, Colombia,
and your memory is buried beneath
a newsman's coifed veneer
again.

Fish eat our eyes, yet we continue
raising our weapons with an anger we were taught.
Our corpses will wash ashore
again and again
to the eyes of children,
sun-caked and sickened.

Little Nutty Bar

1.

The man I love hid the Nutty Bars
from me, citing the inherent
disgust of anyone eating Little Debbie
and my expanding waistline.

For you, he tells me, to help you.
It's not okay, he tells me, to eat those
gross peanut butter wafers covered
in sticky sweet chocolate.

My best friend will balk
at my love hiding food
as though his job were to condition me
into a better version of myself.

She will comfort me as shame
leaves grooves like laugh lines.
I'll shrug it off,
perhaps I am wrong.

Probably I am wrong.
Still, when I find the box,
I devour it whole, burying the shells
at the bottom of the recycling.

2.

I stand in front of the mirror.
Pinching my arms.
Gripping my thighs and jiggling
too hard for comfort.

Delicious the fire that remembers
everything it burns,
as if you could cut open
the flame and inside
find the sediment of desire.

Oh, Little One, I laugh,
I wanted to be you so much,
I've decided to keep you—
to swallow you whole, devourer.

3.

One of my students brings
Nutty Bars to the last day of
class, a potluck I'd declared
to celebrate our writing.

They're so good, she says,
when she catches my eye
consuming the yellow box's
sincere midwestern smile.

I know, I know.
During class I restrain.
Let the cookies and cakes
fill younger, leaner stomachs.

And when they leave—
I sit quietly at the desk in the
corner and peel myself open.
Two bites and poof:

Only the plastic remains,
A tell-tale sign of devouring—
the eager hunger
of one with something to hide.

The Airplane Wife

A gunman in Los Angeles delays all flights.
How a crisis at LAX grounds
our non-Californian locations,
we'll only speculate.

My paramour texts me with
his seatbelt unbuckled.
Bristled in hair and humor.

Selfishly, we worry about losing our Here.
We guard precious time—
these tarmacked hours a tragedy's theft.

I jump into fix-it mode.
Call the airline,
make sure there's a seat
on the next flight.

It takes two minutes,
the woman is cheerful.
They would have done it anyway, she assures.

The Swallows

"He'll be late, but he'll be here—"
I declare to her for no reason at all.
I hear the smile in her voice as she agrees,
He'll be there.

Here is a bag of doubts and nails,
a collapse of time and distance
between coasts and better judgment.

What I don't tell my love:
When she asked my relationship
to the passenger, I hesitated.
Then I said *Wife*. Wife, I said.

Because I knew it'd be easier
to lie for efficiency—
to explain the information and
confirmation codes I kept—
the kind of lie that sounds true for
having said it. Like I Love You.
Or Forever. Or Hello.

His seatbelt will click soon
after I've put down the phone.
I'll try on the word
for a moment—like my mother's
heavy Opium-toned perfume—
and find it too strong for daily wear
just yet.

I imagine all the concerned voices calling

after the shooting. All the airlines
reassuring them that yes, he's
coming, she'll be there.

The scared husband who can't
remember how long his wife's connection
lasted, suddenly swallowing his heart.

The boyfriends, girlfriends, roommates,
and lovers who pretend to be siblings and
spouses, parents and counsel—

ostensibly to fix things,
the lie white enough almost to be transparent
in our quick pauses and strained coughs.

When, I ask, will he finally be here?
Tonight, the airline lady says, *before tomorrow;*
He'll be home.

What I don't tell her:
The house in my voice,
the kin in my relief—

It is a gunman in an airport.
Utterly familiar and terrifying,
the surprise of never
believing the official story.

the origins of the knife war

she put his knives in the dishwasher

he put notes on the dishwasher
to helpfully remind her that knives
most definitely did not go in the dishwasher

no one knows if she saw the notes
before they fell to the ground and were thrown
away by a third party, also unknown

but again with the knives in the dishwasher
this could not stand

this did not stand

the end of the knife war

she stood in the garden
over the hardest clump of soil
wielding two chef knives
like a television ninja

so help me, she screamed,
*so help me, I will plunge these
knives into the ground if you do
not apologize, I will temper the
shit out this blade until you
apologize, so help me, so help me*

please don't, I'm sorry. Please don't.

And she collapsed, knife in each hand,
into a heap of sobs
because she knew he'd only
apologized
to save the knives

For Libertad

The first time one bicycles through back country,
the smells will be unexpected.
Cars filter the road, encasing the driver like a coffin,
preventing olfactory encounters with
grass and concrete, sunlight and rain.
But on the wobbly frame and rusty chain,
the senses cannot help but consume:
> The scent of rotting food and abandoned buildings,
> sweat and sunflowers, horses and dirt.

> It smells like a blue sky.

The aroma of death is unpleasant.
A small armadillo, a crushed cat pushed up against
a railroad track. Fresh or stale, the carcasses
reek the same. In decaying we are all alike.
The raccoon or the deer—the whiff is easy to learn;
the animal inconsequential.

One might recoil from the perfume
of mortality. But it is best, if one persists in cycling,
to simply identify it, move on, and accept that

roadsides cannot help but double as the
occasional burial ground.

This is what it will come down to:
Decaying in a field.
Beyond, a stout woman will pedal and scrunch up
her nose. She'll know death once she smells it.

One cannot forget so singular a scent.

My 91-year-old grandmother prays for death.
This she will tell me on the phone
every time we speak.

Dementia grips her collar like a robber,
Her broken hip forever serenades her to sleep.
This is not life as she previously lived it.
Pills, television, Americans
who yell at her in English

I think it's been long enough, no crees?

I am not one to argue with my grandmother.

THE SWALLOWS

Libertad killed herself in August.
It took me a week to find out.

The one thing about my life I won't miss:
Being me. She wrote that. *I won't miss being me.*
As if she could have been anyone else.

I want to yell *Live. Live.*
But she hated that. She hated
Living. Why would I ask her to do
a thing I know she'd hate.

In the photographs, these women,
they are always smiling—standing
against a rail somewhere overlooking
something pretty,
like a city or a memory of childhood.

these wind-haired women ignoring
the dark shadow of a stranger on a sunny day.

I'll wonder how many pictures exist
where my terror hugs me like nostalgia,
but all one can see is the slight crooked of my
mischief teeth and tequila mouth.

But I misremember:

the day was not sunny,
the cocktails too warm,
even the pool's reflections seem more doctored
than real, like everything else that happened last week—
or was it a minute ago?

Sometimes, I find myself surprised to be alive.
I'll be driving and for a second I'll wonder
how any of this is happening at all.

Daydreaming is for the immortal on the highway.

Soon I'm grateful. For the jolt in my heart
as a trailer zooms by like a vigilante tremor,
the truck's engine drowning
everything but motor and mechanism.

Suddenly I see it:
A big old bike chain,
turning slowly until eventually,
after enough landscapes have bent it beautiful,
the link breaks.

Joan Miró Stares at the Harvest Moon

I saw you on the ceiling,
orange ball. Orb of Nature's Ovulation.

Closed my eyes, stared at the sun,
poked my lids, recorded the colors,
painted them, fell in love with yellow,
divorced green, danced a tulip,
cocked that purpled star,
and thought of the moon as I
smoked a cigarillo like a diaphragm—
strong inhale, that pathetic hopscotch of a lung.

I told her that in Spain, only sculpture cries.
But some kind of pause swelled her sour.
That lunatic is pregnant, orange ball
of empty pickled sky and squiggly intentions,
like my charlie browns learned to foxtrot their way in.

I suppose I will become the fatherland,
that I will not drop the worm because
I made it in an apple,
I can see you—less lonely that you were.

Adriana E. Ramírez

I see you, orb of moon coupled with dusk,
as beautiful—as a piece of mind
dissected and flattened,
waltzing with the oncoming waxing
of everything sacred and orange
like you.

In Which I Tell You About My Morning

In the hospital, I am quiet.
He looks smaller. Broken. Old.

I consider how fat I look in whites.
How skinny he looks in his.

"You look like a model, old man,"
I want to say. But I don't.

He's always maintained my sense of humor
a boxer above his weight class, my laugh a libertine.

Instead I bring him water,
mumble things at the nurses beyond his hearing,

and loudly tell my mother on the phone that
she should come take my place.

I'll relieve you, I say,
as if sitting vigil to the old man's decline
is less work than filling out endless forms.

Adriana E. Ramírez

I want to tell him that his death seems real,
in a way I'd never considered before,
that I'm scared to see him so fleshy and tubed.

That I saw them cut into his spine,
tear through his flesh, and reveal
him made of paper and thread.

That I saw his bones beautiful.
That I can't bury them;
That I can only cradle them as my own.

He tells me I'm too chubby and quiet,
He tells me to bring him more water.

I do all this and hold his hand,
squeeze it harder than I should,
and hope that says I love you enough
without resorting to words.

I see him choke up and turn away.
My eyes say too much already.

Ivy

There are stories I've buried behind the garden wall,
far from sight. The kind of stories
a girl would give good money to forget.

Oh, there are the ones that easily slip from memory.
Bookshelves full of fading tales.
When chanced upon, eager fingers along spines,
nostalgia's kiss tender like a mother's.

The act of disremembering is different.
Like trying to avoid a reflection,
a certain amount of practice is required:
train the eye to eschew contact,
angle the body to escape polished metal,
distract the mind to avert recognition.

I prefer the shovel approach.
Hide the offending story in a sack,
hope it biodegrades, dance upon its grave,
drown the earth around it in whiskey,
erect and demolish edifice above it,
burn what is built and plant flowers anew.

Adriana E. Ramírez

You could say I'm traditional that way.

But the sneaky fuckers,
the ones that don't stay buried;
the ones that confront me on my lawn,
little saplings of memory and grief—
sprouting even as I cut through and tear—
the kind I thought I buried, and what good
is that garden wall anyway?

Some nights I dream the vines grow
into my bedroom, through window and door,
searching for me unconscious, fertile planting ground.
Each tendril reaches out for me, encircles my body,
wraps me slowly, beginning with toes until
I am less body than red-veined ivy, until even
my screams sprout poison instead of noise.

dog and bird discuss flight, what dog remembers

there is a piece of rawhide I once buried
so deep I lost its scent

there are cats I've watched climb
beyond my reach and bite

with wings their bones would crunch
the satisfied grinding of victory

I want so much to be you as I am
to love you as I make you myself

sweet bird—I can hold you tighter
than you've ever been held

tell me how to catch you
tell me how to catch you

Bird and Dog Discuss Taste, What Bird Remembers

I grieve. This is not something most know—
but birds grieve.

I am not afraid to take flight when I have to.
I have been carrion that's come.

Tell me of pepper. Of sneezing,
of wine. Tell me the story of bacon and cream.

I hear the skin is salty,
remind me—what's salty?

I've got a beak made for the eyes,
a crossmark for underbelly.

I cannot taste this broken twig or cracked sorrow—
yet, I can still taste your poison, old friend.

The Celia Cruz Cycle

1. Guantanamera

Yo soy un hombre sincero
De donde crecen las palmas
Yo soy un hombre sincero
De donde crecen las palmas
Y antes de morirme quiero
Echar mis versos del alma

Beautiful Cubana, dress well
we are going out tonight under the moon
in a green dress
i want you green
i want you green with envy so that
you can only scream Azcar!
Beautiful dancer, dress well
run from the revolution and beg
upon your knees when you
kiss soil stained with flag-wrapped boys
Beautiful singer, dress well
lose three kilos, lose nine
one day you will fit in that dress

of your mother's
or better yet: one day the mothers
will dress like you
beautiful voice, sweat through linen
and sing so loud so you can't hear
people talk about you
they called you ugly
and you made ugly the new black
and you made your black sweeter than sugar
Beautiful Salsera
it doesn't matter
I want you to use those four fingers of
of forehead, and like the star that you are
I want you to fight
I want to see you dressed
in orange with a bouquet of green roses
upon your crown of honey hair.
I want you to go
and teach the world how sound
the drums of change
I want, when you are on God's
right hand for you to fight for your people
because that's the only thing you know how to do
rage your maraca, and wear whatever you want,
because you, Celia, are queen
and now I sing for you

Guantanamera, guajira, guantanamera...
Guantanamera ... guajira, guantanamera.

2. The Philosophy of Carnaval

Todo aquel que piense que la vida es desigual,
tiene que saber que no es asi,
que la vida es una hermosura, hay que vivirla.

Stop crying.
Stop crying.
Stop crying.

Realize you're alive. Realize you can breathe.
Take your feet. Put one in front of the other.
Smile.
Eat what you want.
Remember what it is like to starve.
Stop thinking you're alone. You are not alone.
There is always someone. Somewhere.

Life is not always cruel.
There are only bad moments.
Everything else passes.
Realize things can change.
Realize you can change.
Know that even the worst dictator will die.

Also know he has a brother.
Smile.
Put on a good face.
Even when times are bad.
Even when things can't seem to get worse.
Force it. Love it.

Remember what it is like to starve.

Let the hunger push you. Enjoy the hunger.
Hum. Hum so loud you forget where you've been. Look forward to something new.
Move to New Jersey.

Smile.

Dance. Put one foot behind the other. Twirl. Shake.
Shake harder. Shake everything.
Smile.
Life is a carnival. Life is fucking beautiful.

For those that complain forever.
For those that only criticize.
For those that use weapons.
For those that pollute us.
For those that make war.
For those that live in sin.
For those that mistreat us.
For those that make us sick.

Stop crying.
Stop crying.
Stop crying.

Sing.

Ay, no ha que llorar, que la vida es un carnaval,

es mas bello vivir cantando.
Oh, oh, oh, Ay, no hay que llorar,
que la vida es un carnaval
y las penas se van cantando.

We sing our shames away.

3. Rumba in the Jungal!

It's been over ten years and Celia Cruz is still dead.
She was a queen in a world of councils and dictators
When a King was a promoter
and champions were chattel

Ali and Foreman
1974   Rumble   in   the
Jungle
Not yet the D.R. Congo
Just an eight-round main attraction

She danced on a side-stage.
She sang a song in Yoruba
That someone taught her as a child.
She died at 80 in 2003 and didn't look at day over 65
In 1974 she's fifty—   Fifteen   forgotten   years
hidden within her beehive

I like the way her hair is still a natural color
—in the documentary she appears for a mere moment—
but its brown instead of the blues and reds she'd wear later, yet
still red red lips danced to the guttural and diabetic beats.

As if she wasn't Jesus Come For Ya.
As if she wasn't another reminder
that the stages that day were coal dark—
that the balcony seats seemed more bleached

than the mezzanine.
But she was there! She was there!
And she sang a song in Yoruba
She'd been practicing since a child.

(And at least there was a mezzanine)
She was there!
Smaller and swifter   Than the boxers
But no less a fighter for it

Fidel called her a black menace.
Her smile a too joyful tune about escape to yankee fame,
but it's been over ten years since Celia Cruz got
buried in the Bronx   —dirt from Havana
in a box at her breast

She never escaped Cuba, not really.
She never wanted to.
At the funeral
Her cotton-headed husband

sang a song in Yoruba
He knew she'd loved as a child.
They took her body to Miami for a quick adios
and a hundred thousand mourners blew her kisses

whispering guantanameras like Ave Marias
locking their palms and asking for relics
Cubanos, Panameños, Colombianos, Mexicanos, y Gringos
The mezzanine in full force   No   side   stages
needed

It's been over ten years since Celia Cruz died
And I can't believe I never knew she was there
The film lingers on her for a just minute
And for sixty seconds George and Mohammed faded out

under a score of lively drums
purple plumage
A golden microphone embedded in the
greatest of cleavage

Ali won the match, the money, the fame at home.
In 1974, she had been gone from Havana for twelve years
They called her a queen in Zaire   The dancing woman of Cuba
And now—

The gloves the Greatest wore that day
sit in a museum case in Washington—but she was there.
Some nights a voice still booms through Havana
singing a melody in Yoruba   that it loved as a child.

gravity and disappointment

when I finally learned to do a cartwheel
on the balance beam, I executed slowly—
my coach called it stop-motion gymnastics

hand would carefully grip suede-covered metal,
the steadiness of the legs wheeling-cart across body,
muttered tenants of basic physics like prayer

when tumbling and balance demanded more,
the propulsion of torso without a hand on ground,
the paralytic panic decentering my hold—

I couldn't stop imagining my own
death long enough to leave the ground—quitting
this like I had piano and dance before;

this my mother's greatest chagrin—
too clumsy for the ballroom,
too scared for the sky.

Things I Wish Weren't True #1

In sixth grade, a popular boy in school sat me down.
The lunch bell had rung, and he'd asked to speak to me after class.

I'm not sure what I really thought it would be:
a declaration of crush? a question about my math skills?

So serious with his white-boy eyes,
deep and honeyed as his South Texas skin.

He did not smile as he delivered his verdict,
exact in his phrasing and quick to leave.

You stuff your bra too much, he told me.
Everyone knows you just do it for attention.

Years later, I will invent great comebacks.
The most triumphant involved a flashing,

as if seeing my giant junior high boobs would solve my social crises,
make me less awkward and better loved by strangers with bowl cuts.

Haha, I would say, *these are real—*

The Swallows

maybe jump up and down to prove buoyancy.

The popular boy would widen his eyes,
ashamed at doubting the flesh of my tissue.

I still wonder why he did it at all—
if I had been made of just Kleenex and hope,

what did he stand to gain in telling me?
What mockery did he hope to spare me that didn't already exist?

I would ask him all this, if I could do it again,
and he would probably do the same and leave me—

What I did do: ate lunch alone on a bench outside,
crumpled myself invisible within my sweater,

pondered my own paper body, so willing to fold quietly,
like a love note burned before it's read.

Things I Wish Weren't True #2

He started banging the table with his fist.
Arhythmically. The violent stacatto clear.
As if the table's surface was my mouth.

"Tell me," he screamed, "tell me how I ever
hurt a black person by being white. Tell me
how I ever benefitted from being white?
Tell me what affirmative action scholarship
did I get? What government aid went to me?"

His fist continued to bang.
"Tell me!" bang,
"Tell me!" bang.

He was bigger, certainly.
His palms the size of my face.

There is no stopping
a boomerang once you've unleashed it.
Just a matter of waiting for impact.

I know this lesson well.

The Swallows

He was not my first angry white man.

"WHY DON'T YOU SPEAK?!"
I looked at the other men at the table.
Pale as they were silent.

I knew this battle was mine.
That even though they loved me,
the others probably agreed with him,

complicit in their inaction,
gazes searching mine, wondering
what I would say next.

"You don't know my story."
He finally concluded. Proud.
His fist resting on his beer,
my face a burial ground of accusations.

I thought of my twice great-grandfather,
who changed his name to fit in,
married whiter woman to "improve us,"
reshaped his tongue guttural and quick.

I thought of my grandmother,
perpetually praising the recessive in us,
the way we've escaped the darkness
under our fingernails and in the folds of
elbows and knees.

Instead I sipped beer.
Waited for him to leave,
which he soon enough did.

The one that screams loses,
my mother is fond of saying.
But when I looked at the other men,
the ones who did not speak,
I knew that it wasn't true.

He called to apologize within the week.
I did not take it, unwilling to accept
reparations forced on me like his fist.

When I think of the others,
there is a palm-shaped
bang in my throat—
a shock of pilgrims,
searching for a place to pray,
spreading like an untempered plague.

Tlaloc (Casa Frida Kahlo, March 2001)

She wouldn't have prayed to Tlaloc.
That was for her husband.
Instead she wrote letters to her doctor,
doctorsito!, bemoaning yet another way
her body failed her.

In the gift shop where I feast upon her bones,
there is a bite-sized statue to rain god, fertility jester,
malevolent sprite of harvest and blood.
Nothing else Aztec in the store.
I'm horrified for her.

I consider the jocund acquisitions manager,
adding little monster replicas to the order,
at the factory where all things Frida can be purchased—
so when I meet a Canadian who "so gets her" in line
to check-out, I can fully appreciate the irony of history.

I put the god of drowning in my pocket
and lose him by the time I'm out of Coyoacán.
I imagine he has better ghosts to haunt,
better women to demand at the altar.

glitterati

swarovski crystals glimmered on her
she made a splash in sequins
she charmed in a dress
she rocked the fringe
she shined in a designer
she's head-to-toe glamour
she's in a detailed lace number
she's all haute couture
she shimmered in beads

the star
the star
the star
the star
the star
the star
the star
the star
the star

hollywood VIPS take
the party circuit by storm

The Swallows

in sassy show-stopping sparkles

The woman in the hospital
gown puts down the magazine,
hurls it in my lap
as she runs to the bathroom
and retches for five minutes.

I pick it up and leaf through
the pages, admiring the chic
threading on an a-line starlet.

The woman in the hospital
gown comes back for her magazine.
She waits next to me for her
name to be called from a
list behind a glass sliding window.

Oh, yeah, the woman in the gown says.
I'd wear the green one.
The beading is impeccable.
Heavenly.

Like a star.

Deboradora

The summer I am nine,
we mock Deborah.
I stand on the monkey bar,
taller than my June aspirations.

The woman on the street
screams Mango like it's a song,
and I think about why I'm never hungry
in Barranquilla. Always too hot to eat.

Deborah buys mango and ice covered
in leche condensada.
So much for playground tag, I think.
I don't like the climb down.

"Deborah... devora!" the first cry not mine.
We laugh. We laugh. We laugh. I laugh too.
Soon, the chant grows ugly.
DEBORADORA, DEVORADORA.

Deborah cries.
Drops the mango on the ground.

The Swallows

I want to pick it up,
but instead hide it in the dirt.

Devoradora!
Eat the vowels when you say it.
Quickly. Say it quickly.
Swallow the word whole.

Icarus

Call me Icarus.
From the Greek Ikaros.
Meaning Follower,
Meaning, it wasn't my idea,
Meaning, I only flew because I had to.

The number of exteriority, 22, pushes me
toward the stars. It's in my name, you see.
And when combined with my
karmic six, well, hell, I got wings, who said
don't try, right?

I am cautionary.
Don't fly too close to the sun.
We only have wings of wax anyway.

I am ruled by light and water.
Question and answer:
What is it like—raised in a labyrinth?
How hot is it—the sun?

I was born in a woman's deathbed,

The Swallows

My mother slavery.

As for homes without escape,
fates bound by unending hedges,
and the constant threat of a monster,
engineered by gods and family…
well, that was normal. Honest. Real.
Part of the plan from the beginning:
I was taught earth to better understand sky.

Call me Icarus. Flying steady ain't my thing.
Odysseus had it easy. The rock of Scylla.
The hard place of Charybdis. There is a *between*.
Mine was water and fire, the sky betwixt not big enough
for my desire. Ocean and sun.
Both calls much sweeter than dilemma.

What is a boy untested?
What is a boy wearing his father's wings?
What is a boy never kissed, even by sun?

The karmic six, that's all I know.
The weight of obligation, restriction.
Scrupulous. Needy. Wanting care.
Never whole. A boy defined by the man
who made him wings. Hello.

But here's the tickle of the wind
as you feel inevitability's tender caress.

I've flown.

I flapped wings and felt the undercurrent lift me, my body.
I lost touch of ground and hugged sky with my toes.
I've looped stars and breathed in clouds.
I've written my name in your oceans.
I've written my name in your sun.
I've written my name in your breath.

They will tell you that I fell.
That my giddiness overwhelmed me.
That I flew too high. Too close. Too hot.
That I melted. Broken.
Don't do it. Don't flirt with dilemma.
Don't escape a lifetime of confinement
to die minutes from freedom.
to die minutes from a different kind of labyrinth.

Call me Icarus.
From the Greek Ikaros.
Meaning Follower,
Meaning, it wasn't my idea,
Meaning, I only flew because I had to.
Icaro. Hijo de Dedalo.
Icarus son of sun.
Icarus conquerer of sky.
Icarus, boy unleashed from maze,
boy who flew, Icarus
more than caution,
Icaus, myth, Icarus,
who dared touch life at
its origin.

The Swallows

The gods, they watched me fall, indifferent
in their love.

For they know.
This is fate.
This is numbers.
This is constellation.

I fall from the sky. I fall from the sky.
But to fall, but to fall from the sky,
but to fall, I first got to fly.

Eff Mi

Fuck me like I just invented a wet pussy and you are a dying man, crawling through the desert—looking for something to drink and the only thing that will rehydrate your cracked and dry body is my brown girl juice.

Fuck me like I just fired you and the mortgage is due and everything's fucking apart and all you got is my soft pillowcase of a body to keep you from imploding.

Fuck me like the cable company—tell me you're coming soon, that you'll plug in my box, but keep me waiting between eight and twelve until you finally show. Fuck my day.

Fuck me like you're the 1%, like your checking account after Black Friday, like you're kicking the occupiers out of my park in full Storm Trooper Gear. Fuck me like you own Storm Trooper Gear.

Fuck me harder than organic chemistry. Fuck me so hard that I drop you and retake you, over and over again, because I'm just bad remembering the formulas—Fuck me into an English major.

Fuck me like you're a Microsoft product. Like you're a Microsoft support employee. Like there's no CTR-ALT-DLT. Fuck me till my key's rubbed raw.

Better yet—get your metal detector and a snow shovel: we're going digging for my clitoris.

Fuck me like you're a House Republican and I'm a Socialist Black President.

Fuck me like you're two white guys from Oklahoma and I'm a Federal Building.

Fuck me like your wide stance gives you a lower center of gravity.

Fuck me like you're a glue factory and I'm a little pony.

Fuck me like you're the TSA and I'm a seven ounce bottle of lube in your carryon. Confiscate me.
       Relish that shit.

Fuck me like it's legitimate so I can shut it down then fuck me illegitimately so I can't.

Fuck me like my body belongs to the state. And you live off handouts. Fuck me like you got somewhere else to be.

Fuck me like the answer to all your hurt is deep inside me like an untapped well just waiting for you to strike.

Fuck me like you don't like me, like you're trying to feel like a real man, like pulling my hair will somehow make up for all your failures, like my vagina will rebuild your credit score and make you less like your Daddy.

Fuck me like I'm your Daddy Issues. Like all the parts of yourself that you hate can be trapped in that condom.

Fuck me like breathing my sweat makes you drown a little less.

Fuck me and make me promise it meant nothing, fuck me even as you leave.

But, baby, please, it's been a minute.

Just fuck me.

The Naming of Things

1.

When I was four years old,
The night's shadows often
Pulled me from my bed to the next room,
Where my brother fought them for me.

That one, he'd say, that one looks like a bent old tree.
He's Mister Tree. And that one, that one looks like He-man.
And that one—that one is Optimus Prime.

I liked naming things. I still do.
I name characters in fictions I will never write.
Cornelius. Henrietta, Tlacotlaltepetlel
I name clouds and stars. I love the names some already have.
Sirius, Stratocumulous, Ursa

Viruses and bacteria, despots and revolutionaries,
Staphylococcus, Ebola, Idi Amin,
the scientific names of extinct animals,
Raphus cucullatus,
I love the names of streets and old men.

Mellon Terrace, Humphrey McIntlock

My boyfriends freak when I name our potential children.
As do friends, colleagues, and
strangers I meet in line at the post office.

I have names for all my impossible offspring
If I had a baby with the State Of Texas,
I'd name him Wesley.
I think Wesley Texas has a nice ring to it.

2.

My brother is not around anymore,
I like to name the reasons why
Fate and Circumstance.

But I name him Loss instead.
I've lost many things.
I name that Abandonment, Carelessness, and Fear.
I name long nights Loneliness and sad nights Pity.

I name the bags under my eyes
and the curve of my belly Insecurity.
I name myself Lazy, Scared, and the Afraid.

I have written the names in
this imaginary baptismal book
I carry around my neck—Albatross.
I have bathed the letters in holy water,

THE SWALLOWS

weighed each consonant, and called myself Aware.

Yet's easy to see Bleak and Downtrodden.
So I've decided to prove
that the pages of my book look more
a Etch-a-sketch than stone,
that I can rename those suckers.

Uncertainty can become Promise.
Abandonment can be called Transition.
Pity can be called Self-Reflection,
Insecurity? Simply an Abundance of
Raw Material from which I get to sculpt myself anew.
 Scared is also Growth. Fear [is] Living, and Loneliness [is] Learning

I want to rename friends
Life Support Machines,
but that sounds cold and sterile,
so I will rename them Mateys,
because they mostly look like pirates.

I want to take the space in my heart
where Loss lives and rename it Memories.
Call it… The Story of Me.

I want to name my heartaches after hurricanes.
This is Heartache Nimrod.
Level 5 Idiot.

No, I want to call it Metaphor.
to know it is a bridge,

a muscle that links two ideas,
ideas like me, like you, and redefines them as us.

I want to get mixed up in that Metaphor.
And emerge re-sampled,
re-catalogued, re-vamped.

My brother told me names were powerful.
and should be used wisely.
That was all there was to it.
to let go of everything that was wrong.

Tonight, I rename myself Ambition.
I rechristen y'all Daydreamers and Lovers and Wishers and Alive.
If I had a baby with the Future,
I'd name her Adventure.
I'd name her Possibility.
I would name her after all of us.

A Simile Like You

We drive along the highway in Indiana
snow on the ground—sunglassed and pure
like a Tuesday.

And inside my head there's a swelling;
inside my head, shit's about to burst.

There's crises on the left—
    a woman plowed into the pink clay,
    a child forgotten for seven hours at soccer,
    a fat man's scream like a feathered snake
        coated in salt, like a tracked mark—
seconds before we all slide up half-burnt anyway.

Like my eyebrows are fire,
and the lashes small fans
and your eyes, baby,
smell like kindling

What I'm trying to say is that
my facial hair has depreciated,
my left ventricle's been remodeled,

my esophagus got new locks
and my gizzards turned into pie,
cuz no one makes pie sleep on the couch.

And I like you.

Like bananas in underwear,
like television on my skin before breakfast,
like you bought me scissors and a dotted line—
    showed me how destruction meant order
        how sweet fruit, when crushed, can't recover—
            but it always tastes better broken.

Like monkeys watching us at the zoo,
like butter on a pine tree,
like a museum when you kick it,
like a smile on a bitch:
We're improbable.

And I like you like you like me,
like looking liking loves.
But this shit's about to burst.

And teeth that look like daggers usually are.
But I kissed you anyway and I told you
I believed in astrology so you'd give me a moon,
settling for a lunar pod, cuz, hell, the economy's shit and Indiana
is looking more and more like my life
than any other wasteland
these days.

The Swallows

So you were naked and I laughed at you,
called you my little goat monster, but that's just because
beauty is fucking hilarious,
like talking to a face on a magazine
or an advertisement for liquid joy.

But what I meant to say is that you look—
    like all the happymeal toys I coveted as a child,
    like feather, rope, & glue,
    like a computer under water,
    like sanity and ketchup,
like everything else so familiar and impossible and real.
    like blood
    like sandwiches
    like a blind bird sculpted
    like sand
    like my heart in your breaking hand

One day, it'll be us,
two human beings with belly fat
and a keen sense of humor,
actually walking away, like two flirting chasses
passing one another on a highway in Indiana.

For a second, the disco funk dance-track will skip
and my voice, as I sing along, will
hit the one note that makes me thirsty
like a bloody mary for you.

And when I look over,
you'll be gone—

and I'll wonder if you existed, if you stepped out
for fuel and stretch,
your plates clattering as the landscape consumed you
like all the roads we've traveled do.

Baby, this shit burst.
And I wonder if you were ever really there.

Like a bridge after fire.
Like words.
Like/Love.
Like this highway
    in Indiana.

How to Punch Someone Without Getting Hurt

It will always hurt. Don't fool yourself.
But, once you've bloodied knuckles enough,
you will stop feeling.

You will learn to love the ugly.
    Shattered ribs.
    Broken collarbones
    Crooked noses.

That chair, you'll say, I threw it at her
In a fight. That's why it rocks a little.

You will like it better this way.

You always know where you stand
on a broken chair.

When the rage comes, you will
Attempt to quiet it.
You will clench your fists.
You will make yourself small

So that you don't explode harder
As each finger curls under
You'll pray for caution
For patience
For the opportunity to be less
Like your forebearer and his before

When you know you can't contain it
    When the crimson bursts whatever
    Dam kept it abated
When the smile you've been flashing
Turns from insincere to terrifying
    The kind of smile that breaks
    A woman's arm
That's when you will know
    when you will first look for a wall
    a window
    Or any surface that can absorb the shock
    Of your fury

It will surprise you how good it feels
A joy that borders on pride
    Like you made something
    with your hands

When you a hit a person
The feeling will be different.
    It will still you how much more pliant
    Skin is than a punching bag.
    How much easier it cracks
    How much harder

The Swallows

Bones are than wood
    How long you can tornado
    Before you suffocate in marrow

You will regret.
You will beg.
You will promise.

But if you don't.
What will you feel?
Like you've connected to something
Greater than yourself,

Till hurt is just something that   happens
    Something you feel below the wrist   And above the neck.

You were taught
To always put up a good fight

You have got a criminal smile
The kind
That would break a woman's arm
But I've told you that

You will learn to take your licks
    To heal scratch marks
    To apologize to men in uniforms
You will learn
    To make excuses
    To make them understand

Adriana E. Ramírez

That it was never your fault

You will never unlearn how curl your fist
    You will tell them they were wrong
    You will show them they were wrong

You stop feeling
That's how you punch someone without getting hurt

I love you so much that I could hit you
over and over again as you tornado back
Our crooked little dance
until bruises fuse our skin
Until ugly is all that we feel
All that we are

It's a Doggy Dog World

Colonel Dinosaur curls up next to me.
His wet nose soon in my lap,
his schnauzer mustache improbable.

When I ignore him, he doth complain—
his furry eyebrows insistent,
his tongue a quiet alarm
raspy in its metronome.

For a bit, I indulge him,
scratching snout and ears,
his nubby tail stump wagging furiously,
a windshield wiper in monsoon.

Soon I tire. I cannot caress him infinitum.
Like all humans, I cannot love
anything an eternity except in promise.

When I stop, he will sit in protest,
roll over, expose belly—
vulnerable, as all creatures begging love must be.

I offer him a shrug
as Lila and Lola mutt
their way through his
line of sight.

And Colonel Dinosaur leaves me for them—
Because, you know,
Bitches.

About the Author

Adriana E. Ramírez is a Mexican-Colombian nonfiction writer, storyteller, digital maker, and performance poet based in Pittsburgh, where she is writing a book about her death fantasies, the War on Drugs, and the way we tell stories around violence. She teaches in the English Department at the University of Pittsburgh; her intellectual interests include violence, latin america, black markets, code-switching, digital literature, remix culture, video games, confessional poetry, and testimonio—among other things.

Once ranked the 26th slam poet in the world (Individual World Poetry Slam, 2006), she now co-runs the Pittsburgh Poetry Collective (and Steel City Slam) and serves on the Executive Committee for Poetry Slam Inc, while continuing to perform on stages around the country. She was recently featured in the 2014 Legends of Poetry Slam Showcase and TEDxHouston. She also co-founded Aster(ix) Journal with novelist Angie Cruz. Ramírez is a graduate of Rice University (B.A. English) and the University of Pittsburgh (MFA in Nonfiction Writing).

Her writing has appeared in the Los Angeles Review of Books, Guernica/PEN, Convolution, HEArt, Apogee, and Nerve.com. Ramirez is the author of two poetry chapbooks—The Swallows (Blue Sketch Press) and Trusting in Imaginary Spaces (Tired Hearts Press)—as well as the nonfiction editor of DISMANTLE (Thread Makes Blanket Press). She is VONA alum and staff, a perpetually-disappointed fan of Mexican soccer, and a lover of beaches.

She's the winner of the 2015 PEN/Fusion Emerging Writer's Prize, which is given to recognize a promising writer under age 35 for an unpublished work of nonfiction that addresses a global or multicultural issue.

She currently at work on her debut book, The Violence, part family memoir and part journalistic investigation into Colombia and its culture of violence (forthcoming from Scribner, 2017).